The Heart of an Athlete
A Guide to Conquer Mental Blocks

Written By: Jessica Cunningham

Photography By: Natalie Hall

The opinions in this manuscript are solely the opinions of the author and do not represent the opinions or thoughts of the publisher. The author has represented and warranted full ownership and /or legal right to publish all the materials in this book.

The Heart of an Athlete

A Guide to Conquer Mental Blocks

All Rights Reserved.

Copyright © 2015

This book may not be reproduced, transmitted, or stored in whole or in part by any means without the expressed written consent of the publisher except in the case of brief quotations embodied in critical articles and reviews. No part of this document may be reproduced in any way whatsoever without written consent from the author.

ISBN: 13: 978-1507511350

LCCN: 2015912023

CreateSpace Independent Publishing Platform, North Charleston, SC

PRINTED IN THE UNITED STATES OF AMERICA

Dedication

It is hard to acknowledge any achievement of mine without also recognizing my friends and family who have helped me along the way.

To my parents, Ann & Stan Cunningham, thank you for always prioritizing my happiness and sacrificing your time and money so I could be an athlete. Throughout the years, you have believed in me and supported me and I cannot thank you enough. I love you.

Without having coaches who believed in me, I never would have made it as far in gymnastics as I did. Specifically, I would like to thank Heather Humphrey, who consistently guided me with grace and patience. Heather, a portion of my success as a coach is because you loved me as a person and as your athlete. You are the kind of coach I most aspire to be like, and I can't thank you enough for being such a positive role model for me.

After I retired from gymnastics, I started working to help support my husband and myself. Unfortunately, I didn't have time to do anything athletic. But for years, I missed training every day and felt like I was missing something definitive in my life. While on the search to find what I felt I was missing, I stumbled upon Crossfit and immediately knew I had discovered what I had been looking for. Not only had I found an outlet for my desire to be an athlete again, but I was also given a second chance to overcome the mental struggles that I battled as a gymnast. Thank you to my coach, Andy Hamilton for being patient with me and daily pushing me past where I think I can go. The athlete that you are speaks volumes to me and motivates me to work through my mental mess. I truly believe that I am the athlete I am today because of you. Thank you for believing in me and making an effort to know me as an athlete.

To my Crossfit family, thank you for welcoming me in and believing in me when I forget to. You all are an inspiration and I am honored to be able to train with you.

Although I never became a gradeschool teacher like I originally thought I would, I still have the passion to teach. I want to teach because while I'm on this earth, I want to make a difference. One of the most rewarding things for me is to witness growth in people and see them gain confidence and strength along the way. To my team of talented gymnasts at Rigert Elite Gymnastics, thank you for allowing me to be a part of your life. I love you girls as if all 25 of you were my own. Watching your transformation over the past year has been as beautiful as the people you are growing into. I am so proud of each one of you and can't wait to see where your hearts will take you. Thank you for your hugs and always making me laugh. I can honestly say that my life is brighter with you girls in it. You make my job about more than just teaching gymnastics, because to me, you are my family.

Natalie Hall, you really are a fabulous photographer and I am so grateful to have your talent in my book, but also your friendship. Thank you for your enthusiasm and for always being willing to do what you could to help me.

To my dear friends who have encouraged my vision to write this book, thank you for being willing to edit and help put it all together. For fear of missing someone, I won't name names, but you know who you are. Thank you for encouraging me to fulfill my passions and chase my dreams. I love you so much.

Last but not least, thank you to the God of creation who loves me so that I can love others. No matter how big the mental block, I know He will always equip me with new insights and will be there to empower, comfort, and uplift me. I am thankful that He purposefully built me to be an athlete so I can serve the people around me. I will never stop being impressed with what he created me to do. Without Him, this book would not be possible. So from the bottom of my heart, thank you God for everything.

Dear Reader:

If it were possible to sit with you face to face and talk about our shared love for sports and fitness, I would. But since meeting you isn't an option, writing you a book that shares my heart to yours has to be the next best thing. But first before we get into the nitty-gritty, let me tell you a bit about me.

When I was six years old, I started gymnastics and competed from the age of seven to ten. In a few short years, I progressed to level seven, and like most young gymnasts, had dreams of going to the Olympics. After enduring the loss of a family member, however, I quit at age 11 and didn't come back to the sport until I was 18. With a smaller goal to get onto a college gymnastics team, I started training again and competed my way to level ten. Being a high-level gymnast turned out to be a lot different than what I thought it would be. Physically the work was harder, sacrificing a normal life was difficult, and mentally I didn't know how to conquer my fears. Even when I made the decision to retire, I knew I would be back in the gym somehow. In 2010 I found a job coaching compulsory a team and instantly knew I had found my place. I have been coaching ever since.

Alongside coaching gymnastics and my more recent love for Crossfit, writing has always been a passion. Recently I brought that passion to the gym. In August, I started training for the American Ninja Warrior show via Crossfit and got a second chance to be an athlete again. I also re-discovered some of the mental challenges I struggled with as an athlete and started writing about them in journal entries. My initial hope was that I could work through my hang-ups so I could progress, but it dawned on me that my level three team gymnasts could benefit from my process. As we read and discussed my journal entries, I began to see a huge progression in them as they were challenged with different concepts. Their growth was inspiring. Not only did they understand ideas that were years beyond them, they blossom as athletes and as people and I got a front row seat to watch their process. For me, making these connections and making a difference ultimately fulfills why I coach in the first place.

The Heart of an Athlete covers topics ranging from how to handle nervousness to body image. For some of the entries, I have constructed conditioning workouts or specific assignments that reflect the topic of the reading so athletes understand them better. If you are a coach looking to mentally grow your team in this way, follow my blog at www.jessicacunningham.net. I think you will find that mentally preparing your athletes against mental blocks proactively, instead of waiting until mental blocks plague them, will work wonders. I strongly suggest that coaches and/or parents take the time to read through the entries together with their athletes, making sure to stop often for the sake of comprehension. Set aside a time to enjoy the bonding that comes with mentally training your athlete to succeed. To the athletes, know that I believe in you and hope that from this book, you are able to gain insights that help you become even more amazing than you already are!

Yours Truly,

Jessica Cunningham

Table of Contents

1) A Learning Curve

2) Commitment

3) The Right Focus

4) Waiting

5) Staying in the Present

6) Muscle Memory

7) The Wall

8) New Limits

9) Nerves

10) No Gymnast is an Island

11) The Standard

12) Perfection

13) Self-Sabotage

14) The Nurturer

Table of Contents

15) Fight or Flight

16) Negativity

17) Struggles

18) The Ugly Truth

19) Insecurities

20) Score Chasing

21) The Pain of Change

22) Another Me

23) The Why

24) Loving the Journey

25) Swimming in the deep end

26) Belief and Confidence

27) Photo Gallery

A Learning Curve

A Learning Curve

I have a list. Of things I want to do and experience at least once. Some of the things that are on my list include the following: Write a novel, learn to play an instrument of strings (either the guitar, violin, or cello), high kick up to my face, find true friends I can be myself around, sing in public, get stronger, and choreograph a ballet/modern dance routine that expresses emotion. Most of the things on my list require learning and practicing in some form, which means that I won't start out as good as I want to be. For some reason, I expect to be a professional right away, so for me, being a beginner is a hard concept to accept. Actually, I would say it is the one thing that stops me from starting to learn new things at all.

When I first decided I wanted to write, for a long time I didn't. I had no problem talking about my intentions, but when it came down to sitting and writing, I couldn't. There was always a reason why it didn't work out. I wasn't comfortable enough, or I didn't have enough time, or I was too tired, or I wasn't in the right place. Even if there wasn't a reason, sometimes I still couldn't bring myself to write. I remember being so frustrated feeling like I was a prisoner in a cell to my own inability, because more than anything, all I really wanted to do was get out of my head and write. After months of failed attempts, a good friend finally came to my rescue and challenged me to write like garbage. His advice surprised me because it wasn't what I was expecting. His instructions were to produce the worst piece of writing, so long as I wrote something down. At first, my writing was terrible. I found that the most difficult part of this process was letting go of the expectation I put on myself to be unrealistically good at something new. As I began to write more often, my ability began to come through and eventually I became more confident in my own voice as a writer.

This idea I have to be instantly great is motivating, but what I learned is that whenever you learn something new, you have to go through a turbulent period where you allow yourself to be bad before you can ever be great. You have to go through a learning curve. If you are willing to go through the process from beginner to expert, no matter how long that takes you, you will appreciate the journey more than if you didn't have to work for it at all. In the end, you will have come out stronger for enduring the wait. Before you know it, you will be able to look back and see how far you've come, and you will have accumulated a list of different things you have conquered while learning. What better proof do you need than to be able to recount the things you have overcome? Sometimes regardless of what holds you back, when you are learning something new, the most important thing you can do is start.

Reflect

Think about a time you tried something new. In the beginning, were you a professional? How long did it take for you to get better?

How does it make you feel when you can tell that you are getting better?

Commitment

"Commitment means staying loyal to what you said you were going to do long after the mood you said it in has left you."
—Unknown—

Commitment

By definition, commitment is thought of as being consistent or following through with your word. While those definitions are correct, for athletes, commitment goes beyond loyalty. Whether you are a beginner in any sport or a professional, much of your success is determined by how much effort you put into what you are doing. If you want to progress, you must do more than show up and go through the motions. You have to make a commitment to work hard and consistently give 100%.

When I was young, I didn't really comprehend being committed to the way I was training until I was challenged. Most things came easy to me, so I didn't have to try my hardest. Don't get me wrong, I struggled, but mostly because I wasn't ready to commit emotionally, mentally, spiritually and physically to what I was attempting to do. To be a successful athlete, you have to commit in all areas, or else your career will fizzle to retirement in a hurry. This kind of commitment is a lot to ask of someone. Anyone can just show up, but not everyone is willing to put 100% effort into what they are doing. Honestly, it's easier not to try your hardest, but progress lives off of full commitment. In short, it comes down to this question:

How badly do you want it?

It takes a strong person to fully commit to anything or anyone. Along the way there are bound to be bumps and setbacks that might delay the arrival time of your goals. Running into setbacks is usually what makes people turn from their plans, but holding yourself accountable, no matter what, will teach you about who you are and what you can achieve when you stick it out. A lot can be discovered by someone who stays committed to trying their best and who puts their heart into everything they do. At the end of the day, the individuals who choose to train this way will find that struggling to commit was worth it. Consistently training your hardest will bring big results faster than going through the motions ever could.

Trying your hardest is a strange concept because it brings a delayed reward. Doing it once won't always produce immediate results. What will produce results, is trying your best on every skill you do, every day, even on the days you don't want to. Trust me, there is nothing more reviving that blooming with success because you did. Whether or not your commitment to quality training brings you a medal or trophy, there will always be something to be proud of. That makes your time in the gym well spent.

Reflect

How often do you put 100% effort into your training?

What stops you from trying your hardest?

When you catch yourself giving less than 100%, it might be helpful to ask yourself why and mentally re-start. This will help you re-focus and train better. What could you do to mentally restart?

The Right Focus

"When you focus on problems, you'll have more problems. When you focus on possibilities, you'll have more opportunities."
-Kushrandwizdom-

The Right Focus

For the most part, I consider myself to be a focused person. It depends on what I have my mind set on, but when I get in the zone, I am downright stubborn about getting something finished. I've noticed that when I am training, I put a lot of concentration into every movement I do. Sometimes that's a good thing, like when I need to focus on a certain part of a skill, but other times it holds me back because of the way I am thinking about what I am trying to achieve. The past couple of weeks, I've learned an interesting fact about what it means to focus. Focusing can be just as hurtful as it can be helpful. When you're trying to progress, you can be focusing on the very thing that is holding you back. It's easy to cross that line without even knowing. By focusing on things like fears or what not to do, you are feeding a negative thought and before you know it, you are doing the very thing you wanted to avoid.

To prevent falling off the beam, I used to tell myself not to fall. In my attempt to stay on, I would tense up and ultimately fall anyway. I remember getting so frustrated when I did this, because I thought I was doing everything I could to stay on the beam, but by tensing up, I was only locking my muscles into place. Thinking about not falling caused me to stiffen up to the point that I wasn't able to use my muscles the right way, making it impossible to keep myself from falling. It took me a while, but eventually I learned how to concentrate on relaxing to absorb my landings instead of freezing up. To my surprise, relaxing proved to have other benefits as well: I was able to focus more clearly and I was more aware of where I was in a skill. I found that if a correction needed to be made, I was able to make it before I started to fall.

My entire life gymnastics has almost been about luck, because my focus was always on what I didn't want to happen. Sometimes executing my skills was a shock to me because I expected to fail. There were several competitions where I walked away wondering how I made the skills that I did because my only thoughts were of how upset I would be if I didn't make them. I know my mind is able to achieve anything I want, but maybe my mind is what has been getting in the way this whole time. Maybe my body would be able to reach higher heights if my mind didn't focus on the worst case scenario. What if I focused more on neutral things, like keeping an even pace between movements, or finishing each movement before thinking about the next one? What if, when in the middle of a skill, I could focus on what I need to do to be successful instead of what I don't want to do. How much further would I be able to go?

Learning to have the right kind of focus is key. It's where your power is hiding, it's where your true capabilities are waiting. Learn to wield it, and you become boundless.

Reflect

Take a moment to think about a skill. When you do this skill, what do you usually think about?

Instead of what not to do, what can you think about instead?

Waiting

"Re-visit your basics often. Without them, you wouldn't be able to put anything together."
-Jessica Cunningham-

Waiting

If you are an athlete, you have probably been involved in your sport for a long time. Part of what makes any sport so tough is the dedication it takes to spend all your time in the gym. Day in and day out you work to improve your speed, strength, and flexibility and courageously work to do what most people only dream of doing. In addition to all that, it is also your job to study and master each skill you do. When I was in training, it was hard for me to master certain skills because I didn't understand the timing they required. If my coaches told me what shape I needed to be in or what shape I was forgetting, my question was always "When?" While that was an important question, there was something even more important that I was missing.

Most of the time when attempting a skill, I would skip a certain part because I just wanted to get to the main ingredient. Whether that was flipping, twisting, or jumping, I was always a beat too early. Slowing my skills down was hard for me because I was afraid I would not make them if I executed them too slowly. What I didn't recognize was how high I was in the air when I attempted to make the skill in the first place. I failed to see that I had set the skill up for success in the beginning, but got impatient. I would often misjudge the reality of where I was in the air and ruin my attempt at making it by rushing through steps or skipping them all together. In my mind, timing was what I made it. I thought the slower movements were for the smaller skills and the faster movements were for the bigger skills. To some degree I was right, but not completely.

You see, all skills have a unique pattern to them. While they are governed around the laws of gravity and physics, there are shapes, rhythms, techniques and different speeds that make every movement a success. Some skills can go quick-quick-slow or slow-quick-quick or quick-slow-quick or slow-quick-slow. It all depends on what the skill requires of you. It's strange to think about, but most of the skills I mastered happened because I set them up with all of the power that I had, and then I let the timing of the skill carry me the rest of the way.

Knowing the timing of a movement or a skill is what creates efficiency. Efficiency means that you accomplish something with the least amount of effort and the most amount of proficiency you can. A lot of the time when you skip the steps in your skills, you end up making more work for yourself. Being an efficient athlete looks like going through the basic steps and learning them well enough that you don't forget them while executing a skill. When it was the last thing I wanted to do, sometimes I had to go back to the basics in order to add them to whatever skill I was working on. Reminding myself what was before the main ingredient always helped me find better success. Every skill after all, is made up of small parts that all require mastery in order to master them.

I eventually got to the point in my training where the word I repeated to myself the most was "wait." My technique and power was there. All I needed to do was wait for the timing to come to me and hit all the steps along the way. For me, it was less important that I controlled the timing than that I waited for it to come naturally. The only thing I had to do after that was trust that the right timing would lead me through. And after putting my basics into my skills, it always did!

Reflect

Describe a time when you rushed a skill.

Sometimes it is easy to rush skills because you haven't practiced the basics enough. When you go back to the basics, you will find out what part of the skill you are missing. How well do you know your basics?

When you don't understand the timing of a skill, have someone record you doing it, or have someone show you what you need to do. This is only one way to learn. Everyone learns differently. What would help you understand your skills better?

Staying in the Present

"When I am focusing the whole world fades away. I am free to be bold, brave and beautiful."
-Jessica Cunningham-

Staying in the Present

It seems I have spent my entire life staying busy. In high school I competed in multiple sports and activities at the same time. I went to youth group once a week, stayed up late doing homework and somehow managed to squeeze in a social life between doing my chores and working on the weekends. Since high school, life for me hasn't really slowed down much. If anything, it has gotten worse- to the point that it is difficult for me to get done everything that needs to get done. Most days I feel like there are simply not enough hours. While keeping active is a good thing, I've noticed that when I have free time, it's hard for me to relax because I can't stop my mind from racing. When I was an athlete, I struggled to slow down my thinking the same way I struggled to slow down my life outside the gym.

I remember having what I can only describe as "blackouts," where I would mentally lose track of what my body was doing while it was in motion. Blacking out this way caused a lot of fear for me because, in the middle of a skill, I didn't know where I was. It was like I was a human torpedo flying through the dark. Not all my skills felt like this. In fact the ones I was mentally in control of, I wasn't afraid of at all. The few times I successfully controlled my mind to focus on what was happening in the middle of a skill that scared me are now memories I will never forget.

"But wait..." You're probably asking, "How did you do it?"

That's a good question. I honestly would never have learned how to do this without my Coach Heather. She knew how hard it was for me to slow down and often challenged me to physically feel every part of every skill I did. After several months of her telling me to stay in the present, I started to think about what that meant. Over time, I realized that staying in the present meant that I stopped trying to control everything and let my body move through space. When I did this, it was as though everything switched to slow motion. Sometimes I didn't have sight of where I was in the air, but because I was letting my body move while mentally keeping track of it in slow motion, I knew exactly where I was.

Although mentally slowing down like this wasn't something that I mastered, it is something I have found to be plenty useful, both as an athlete in Crossfit and as a person trying to embrace the beautiful moments of life. If I could visualize what slowing down looked like to me, I would do it like this:

When I close my eyes and forget where I am, a warm sun begins to glow behind a mountain of green. Gradually, it gets brighter as the river I am on floats me closer to it. I stand in my boat to see what is around the bend. Inch by inch my face is exposed to the sunlight calling me. I take the arm of the wind and dip my toe into a body of water that shimmers silver, like the stars twinkle in the night. At first the sharp coldness alarms me, but also refreshes me at the same time. From behind me, a rush of auburn colored leaves are escorted by the wind, and fly around me until I am surrounded by a whirl of my best soul-mate friends. The moment is so beautiful, I forget what I came here to find. In fact, I am so caught up in enjoying the moment, I don't remember at all. While drawing in a deep breath, I feel joy and peace. Contentment flows from me, and I want to dance in response. Lost in a secret world of my own, I dance in the river deep in a canyon that echoes the words of my heart. This divinity can be described as nothing more than purity in its truest form. It is tranquility fueled by fire. It is freedom that refuses to be tamed. It is the dazzling art of staying in the present.

Reflect

What does staying in the present mean to you?

What does staying in the present look like to you? Describe a picture of what that looks like.

Muscle Memory

"If I trust my strengths more, than I will have less of a need to question what I can do."
-Jessica Cunningham-

Muscle Memory

The more I am around athletes, the more I realize just how incredible these people are. Just when I think the limit has been reached on what athletes can do, someone breaks through and sets a new record. When I see people do this, I can't help but wonder how they achieve so much. In the past month, the main correction I have heard from my Crossfit coach isn't about my form or technique. When my form and technique is all I am thinking about, my coach says to shut my brain off, and move. At first, I didn't think that was a good idea. Like most gymnasts tend to be, I am very analytical and I overthink everything. It's obvious that you need to be thinking about something during a skill, but not to the point where you can't function properly.

The brain has many functions. One of them is to carry specific messages to the body to do different things. Overthinking, however, is when your brain gives your body specific directions, and the message never leaves your brain. With your brain holding onto the message, your body doesn't do anything, because it didn't receive any orders. I think the main reasons athletes overthink is because they are either afraid, or they're trying to make everything too perfect. When they should be almost checking off the list of what needs to be done during a skill, they check, and re-check it over and over again.

Sometimes I forget my own strengths. I train 4-6 days a week and am the strongest I have ever been. My endurance is getting better, my body is hurting less, and my form on my skills are easier to manage. There is no doubt in my mind that I am getting stronger, but still, when I am facing a workout that requires me to rely on my strength, my mind doesn't allow me to. It's as simple as trusting my body, but instead I overthink and keep my body from doing what I have conditioned it to do. The brain and what it can do amazes me, but the extent that it holds me back is also surprising. In my training lately, I seem to get to a point where my brain tells me to settle for how much effort I am putting into my skills. When I start to get a little bit tired, it's like my brain tells my muscles not to go beyond where I am. I kick myself when I listen, because after I'm done working out, I regret not trying harder. My body could have handled it.

Although I am still learning, turning off my brain doesn't mean that I think about nothing when I am training. It simply means that I trust what I have been taught and trust that my body can do what my brain is telling it to do. If I trust my strength more, then I will have less of a need to overthink whether or not I can do something. Sometimes I think my overthinking is productive because it takes a lot of work, but I have found that while it takes a lot out of me, I'm not getting as much physical work done. These are the times when my coach has to remind me to think less. It feels like I am working hard, but in reality I am just wasting time. When I turn off the part of my brain that likes to overthink, I get to see what my body can do, and I am usually surprised. I actually do my best work when I think less and move more. After proving to myself that I can handle more than I thought, the things my brain used to tell me not to do becomes less and eventually turn into muscle memory. If I am ever going to exceed my limits, I am going to have to stop overthinking and give my body a chance to prove that it can be trusted. Defying my brain this way will be difficult, but if a breakthrough to the next level is going to happen, it is necessary.

Reflect

In your sport, what are your strengths?

Describe a time when you got stuck because you were overthinking.

Name three things you overthink the most. Instead of focusing on them, think about your strengths instead.

The Wall

The Wall

So you're in the beginning of your conditioning workout and you are feeling good. You're keeping an even pace and the numbers you are repping seem tangible enough that you are able to do them without stopping. Your heart is beating fast and the energy you're putting out is proven by the sweat that is running off your forehead. Your muscles are fatigued, the workout is hard, but fortunately at this point, you're done. With the first round. Suddenly you realize that you have three more rounds to go and you don't know how you will get through it. As you are thinking more and more about this daunting journey ahead of you, you begin to doubt yourself and you slip into a mindset of paralyzing shock. You tell yourself things like "Maybe I can't," or "It will take a miracle if I can," Or flat out, "There is no way!" Without knowing, you create a mental environment of anxiety and the perfectionist in you starts to panic. Before you know it, you have hit the wall and are unable to move it.

As an athlete, I struggled believing in myself every day. Especially if I had to work hard at something that challenged me. I would start questioning if I was supposed to tackle it. I expected it to come easy. Some skills did come quickly to me, but not all of them. Being a gymnast for so long, you would think I would know how hard gymnastics would be, but for some reason, when I hit my wall, the thing that puzzled me the most was that I was struggling at all.

Sometimes I look in the mirror, and I see an average me looking back. I see someone who has goals and intentions that may or may not be fulfilled. But other times I see a glimpse of a me who is everything I thought I could never be, who has already become the person I want to be. Honestly, it makes me a little uncomfortable to see that, but what if that side of me really existed. If she did, that would mean I could train with her fire and her strength. When you reach this point of self-discovery, it's time to leave the old you behind and push forward with this new-found confidence that will lead you to an unlimited period of goal breaking.

For me, pushing past the wall is a daily struggle. Sometimes it takes time for me to realize that I am holding myself back. Then I remember that I have a hidden confidence buried deep within, that can only be released if I am willing to dig through the garbage that covers it. If I never found this part of me when I was a gymnast, I would never have gone as far as I did in gymnastics, and I would never have reached past what I thought I was. So my question to you is:

Who is it that you say you are?

Find him or her and stop squandering him or her with a you that can only take you so far.

Whatever your goals are, know the journey will be difficult. Expect it to be more difficult than you ever thought it would be and face the difficulties head on with the part of you that is strong enough to break down that blasted wall that hinders you!

Reflect

When you look deep inside yourself, what do you see?

What would it feel like to get past your wall?

What can you do to get past your wall?

New Limits

"Reshape possibility by making the impossible the foundation from where you will launch to reach your dreams."
-Jessica Cunningham-

New Limits

Never in my wildest dreams would I imagine how difficult it would be to mentally train for a physical goal. More than pushing my body to the limit, I am breaking through the set limitations that my brain has created for me. When I am trying to set a new record, it's not an optional fight; it is a mandatory fight to create new capabilities for myself and go beyond what I think is my breaking point. Some people think that curiosity is a bad thing because it opens doors to things you may not be ready for. But then again, how will you know unless you take the risk to find out?

I am learning that I am curious. In secret, I want to know the maximum that I can handle. I want to know how far I can go in every direction. Think about it, if everyone stopped pushing when their brains told them to, how would anyone ever achieve their dreams? The kind of success someone can have, I mean the kind that keeps going when all you really want to do is give up, is unfathomable to us because we believe we can only do so much. Usually, we can do more than we think we can. Exceeding your limits is more than doing your best. It surpasses working hard, or never giving up. It's more like you are re-shaping possibilities, making the impossible the foundation where you will one day launch from to finally reach your dreams.

This changes everything. Things I shouldn't be able to do, things I am too afraid to do, things other people don't think I can do. They are all invitations to overcome. And the sweat that pours, the moments when all I want to do is stop, the burning sensation that surrounds my muscles, the abnormal rhythm of breathing, the question of what will happen if I don't stop. They are symptoms of becoming more than I thought I was. Like never before, anything really is possible.

Reflect

If there wasn't anything holding you back, what would you accomplish?

What are some of the things that hold you back?

When you want to give up, what keeps you going?

Set your New Limits here:

_____

_____

_____

_____

_____

_____

_____

_____

_____

Nerves

"Regardless of how nervous you are to compete, remember that there is a brief window before you begin where you can choose to be in control of what happens."
-Jessica Cunningham-

Nerves

Before a competition, not knowing how you will perform tends to fuel an overwhelming nervousness that often threatens to take over the mind of many athletes. When you train tirelessly every day for one competition that doesn't end up going your way, it's hard not to be disappointed about your mistakes. The whole point of competing after all is to execute as few mistakes as possible, so when you fall short of your expectations, you are immediately filled with regret. Wishing you could have performed better is the worst feeling because you can't do anything about it. Regardless of what you are capable of, or what you usually do in training, what's done is done.

I can remember a competition, where I competed my round off back handspring double pike for the very first time. Even though I had been landing it consistently in practice, I was nervous. I knew I was going to do my best, but I didn't know what that would look like because I couldn't control my nerves. I was confident the dance pose before my big tumbling pass, but somewhere between my first step and my back handspring I started to doubt myself. Just when my ability to focus was starting to fade there was a voice from the crowd that penetrated my nervousness and reminded me to jump, flip and pull like I had been doing in practice. The voice was from a former coach. Hearing her cheer for me taught me something.

Before a specific skill or routine happens, you are in control of that skill or routine. Nervousness is normal, there is no getting away from it. But being nervous doesn't mean the skill you're nervous about won't be good. It just means that what you are attempting to do is important to you and that you want to do well. The moment before you compete, remember that you can still be in control of whether or not you will succeed. Although staying in control of your nerves is not an easy thing to do, every competition teaches you how to manage them a little better. So when you're standing at attention with butterflies in your tummy, most likely questioning how you will perform, remember that despite your nervousness, there is a brief window before the moment happens, where you can choose to be in control and make something good happen.

Reflect

After competing today, what did you learn about yourself?

What did you do well?

Based on your performance, what goals do you have for your training?

No Gymnast is an Island

No Gymnast is an Island

One of the interesting things about gymnastics is that it is a team sport just as much as it is an individual one. The benefit of this set up is that it takes some of the pressure off you if your weak event is your teammate's strength. In general however, it's rare to be successful alone while journeying to your dreams. Every athlete needs a supportive team. The way I see it, we were all born to be social and connect with others. It's only natural to have times when you need to be alone, but only temporarily because any extended period of isolation can bring destruction.

Some people struggle to let their guard down and ask for help. They want to do things by themselves so badly they end up pushing others out. They don't realize it, but the more they resist help, the more they will continue to struggle. Why do we this? Maybe it's because we believe needing help proves we are weak, or that we don't have what it takes to accomplish a goal. Whatever the reason, it's not true. The truth is that everyone has different gifts and strengths, and the areas that are weak are places someone can help you strengthen.

In team sports, your teammates help you to keep going during conditioning when all you want to do is stop. They cheer you on when you need that extra breath of energy during a performance. And most importantly, they catch you when you start to fall into even a second of doubt. That's what makes you a team. You stand together as one unit with many different gifts, and you support each other through thick and thin. That's what makes you a beautiful team. If you're willing, your weakness can become your strength simply by letting someone else in.

When you let others in your head and your heart, you will soon discover that their strengths are contagious. As you work towards your goal with them, eventually your weakness will no longer be your weakness anymore. A good teammate is willing to sacrifice what it takes to be their best, but a great teammate is someone who lifts others up with their strengths and allows their weak spots to be molded by their team.

If you can be this,

Together, you will stand as champions.

Reflect

Describe a time when a teammate helped you.

Describe a time when you helped a teammate?

It is safe to say that athletes wouldn't be able to achieve as much if not for their coaches, friends and family. Who are the people that support you?

The Standard

51

The Standard

Do you ever feel out of place because of the way you look? Or embarrassed because you're body doesn't look like everyone else's? I do. Just like girls get self-conscious about not being in shape, I, as an athlete get self-conscious about being strong. In our culture today, the standard of what girls should be has been loudly communicated to us through magazines, T.V., music and more. According to these sources, girls are supposed to be weaker than boys, have tiny waists and just the right amount of curve, meaning not too much or not too little. If any one of us falls outside this ridiculous standard, we get self-conscious about ourselves and become ashamed of what we are.

Although I struggle with feeling like I don't exactly fit the standard, I hate the fact that there is an expectation like this. When people see an athlete who has a visibly strong physique, or a different build altogether, people respond in different ways. Some of these responses include judging the athlete, feeling intimidated by them, putting the athlete down, or sometimes people are inspired. The truth is, that it doesn't matter what anyone else thinks. In fact I feel bad for the people who judge others, because it tells me they have no idea what true beauty is. They are stuck seeing people in the narrow-minded way our world has taught them to see. Right now I'm learning that being strong says a lot of great things about you. It is a testament to who you are as a person. I'm not strong because I want people to compliment me. I am strong because I face my weaknesses in the gym, because I work through fear and physical exhaustion, because I never give up, and because I believe in myself. I earn my body type as a result of doing these things.

I was made to be an athlete. Like most athletes, my body thrives when it is being pushed. Not only is being an athlete something I am good at, it is something I like to be good at. It is freeing to know I don't have to be what the standard says I have to be. Instead I can just be me. It's important to be comfortable with who you are and what you look like because there will always be someone or something in life that will make you feel inadequate. If you are strong enough to accept your own beauty, your world won't be rocked when someone challenges you.

So whether you hate how strong your legs are, or you get weird when someone notices how strong your arms are, learn to love what you have and use your strength to inspire those around you. Trust me. The world needs to be inspired by you!

Reflect

Have you ever felt out of place before?

What makes you stand out? If you could give a reason why you were born with a different build, why would that be? For me, I was born strong and petite. Most my life I didn't like my small stature, but later discovered that it was perfect for gymnastics. What makes you perfect for your sport?

How can you inspire others to be more comfortable with the way they look?

Perfection

"Never stop working to reach Perfection."
-Jessica Cunningham-

Perfection

Does it really exist? There are many people who think negatively on the concept of perfection. The rumor is that perfection is not attainable and that no one can be perfect. I understand why they say that, but I think they are wrong.

In every sport, there are specific techniques that must be used in order to achieve success. The better the technique, the better the outcome. In gymnastics, for example, every skill is worth a certain amount of points and is written a specific way. Among other things, skills are influenced by gravity, physics, form, technique, speed and amplitude. It's difficult for gymnasts to do, and not all of their attempts will be perfect, but there is such a thing as completing a skill with no error or deduction. A lot of people believe that being perfect is a myth or that it's too big for anyone to reach, so they shy away from it. The problem with that kind of thinking is that it quickly turns into an excuse not to try. Technically speaking, perfection only means that you have no flaw throughout the execution of a skill. The concept is that simple.

Does trying to be perfect mean that you will never fail? NO! But remember this: If the quality of your training is your priority, than the quality of your skills will improve. Let's say you aim to perform a flawless skill or routine and you miss. You are still on the right track because you were not afraid to try to perform the skill or routine perfectly. If you fall trying to be perfect, you are still above those who, on a daily basis, don't prioritize good form or are not willing to try to make their skills perfect in the first place.

For many athletes, trying to be perfect can be frustrating when that's all you want to be. In fact, I've seen it drive people crazy, but I don't think you become perfect just because you're chasing after perfection. Rather than something that you are, perfection is something that you do. If you train with excellence and expect quality training to teach you, then the skill you are working on will soon become perfect. As you understand the feeling, timing, and shape of every skill you do, you can start raising the bar on your capabilities because you were willing to create a good habit through the way you chose to train. Although perfection might seem like it is UN-reachable, if it didn't exist, why would anyone chase it at all. Regardless of what others may think about perfection, be courageous and train with this quote in mind:

No deduction

Be the exception

Work hard to reach your perfection.

I dare you.

Reflect

Choose a skill in your mind. Have you mastered it perfectly? What part of that skill needs work? Once you have found something you still need to work on, don't take the fact that it's not perfect personally and don't be afraid to admit you're not perfect. Instead, get right to work and put in the time it takes to be better.

Think about your last practice or training session. Did you train with excellence? How could you have trained better?

Self-Sabotage

"Self-sabotage is like a game of mental tug-of-war. It is the conscious mind versus the sub-conscious mind where the sub-conscious mind always eventually wins."
- Bo Bennett-

Self-Sabotage

Have you ever wanted something so badly, you would do anything to get it? You want it so much that you are willing to sacrifice everything to capture that dream and make it more than just a dream. So you do everything that dream requires of you. But when you finally get to where you wanted to go your whole life, you can't. Mentally, it's like an invisible wall is standing in the way of you and your goal. After all the work you put in, how can this be? Why is crossing this line so difficult?

When I was young, I knew I wanted to be extraordinary because I felt it in me. I didn't know what I would be good at, but I knew I would l be great at something. Until I found my passion, I tried a lot of sports and instruments that I thought I would be good at. Some of them I was pretty good at, but my heart didn't love them. On the other hand, when I walked into the gym and held onto those bars, I knew right away that I could be good on them. I immediately wanted to learn everything because I believed I could do it. For me, finding gymnastics was my first magical moment because it was the first time I fell in love.

Even though you love them, sometimes sports don't go right all the time. Throughout my career I have had many trying days when I didn't feel like the athlete I wanted to be. Some days were horrific. If I didn't love it so much, those days probably would have driven me to give up. Before I found gymnastics, I did give up on other things I thought I wasn't good at, but I wonder sometimes what I would have become if I had stuck with some of them. Granted, my heart wasn't in them, and I didn't feel as strongly as I did about gymnastics, but in general, I think giving up is something I often default to, because it's easy to do. But maybe there is more to it than that.

I think we, as athletes stop ourselves when we get too close to our goals because we don't believe we are allowed to go beyond them. In other words, we don't believe we are good enough. When we picture the athletes who are at the top of our sport, we don't envision ourselves at their level when we could be. Until we give ourselves permission to reach out and touch our goals, we choose not to.

Maybe some of us are afraid of what will come after we reach our goals. Maybe we are afraid nothing will come after. That after our long journey, there will be nowhere else to go, no other dream to keep our hearts beating. Then what? For some of us, it's almost like we start grieving the possibility of losing that dream before we lose it. So we sabotage ourselves, making it impossible to arrive to it. Following a dream is what wakes us up in the morning and keeps us going. It's a scary thought, but what would we become without them?

Thankfully, dreams inspire more dreams. Just because our narrow minds can't fathom what is beyond ourselves, doesn't mean there is nothing left for us to dream. I think there is an ocean out there filled with rich dreams and even richer moments that will sustain us. Made for everyone in our different phases of life, our hearts will always have what they need to keep going. To some extent, we must believe this, because why else would we dream in the first place? Like water is for our bodies, dreams were given to us because they are a necessity. We just have to choose them.

Reflect

What athletes do you most admire/look up to? Why?

Do you believe you could be as good as they are?

When you reach your goals, you get to start chasing new ones. What might come after achieving your most recent goal?

The Nurturer

"Resiliency isn't
Instinctual, it's
learned from the
people who truly love
and support you."
-Jessica Cunningham-

The Nurturer

Everyone who has a parent, or someone they love like a parent, knows that their influence is essential. When you are a child, you don't know how the world works. You look to your parents for advice, explanations, and the difference between right and wrong. Whether you are aware of it or not, you study how they handle life, and soon their habits, and sometimes parts of their personality, become part of who you are. This is why the role of a parent is so important. They are the main reason why we are who we are.

Specifically when you were a child who fell down and scraped your knee, what was the first thing you did? You probably looked to your parents to see what their reaction was. If they were freaking out and running over to pick you up, you most likely decided the situation was worth crying over. But if your parents were slow to panic and assured you that you were ok, you learned that the fall wasn't that bad after all, or at least that you weren't dying. What about when someone hurts your feelings or when you just have one of those awful days where nothing goes right? On those horrible, bad days, who is it that comes to your side and calms you down? The things they tell you in these moments are the same things you will tell yourself when you get hurt in the future and they're not around. You will follow their example and comfort yourself like they would do if they were there.

Although the relationship between a coach and an athlete is a bit different, it's the same in sports. In the gym, coaches assume the same position as parents. They make sure we are safe, they cheer us on from the sidelines and they keep us together when we fall apart. When it comes down to it, our coaches know us better than we sometimes know ourselves. If not for their care, we, as athletes, would not be able to achieve as much as we do.

For reasons unknown, many athletes have random freak-out moments where they are afraid to do things they are more than capable of doing. But occasionally, they freak-out because of a fall. While retrying the skill they just fell on, it is common for athletes to panic, being afraid to fall again. When the panicking escalates, an overwhelming sensation of defeat covers the athlete and soon they are paralyzed. On many different occasions, I have been this athlete. When I was a gymnast, there were days where it didn't matter what my coaches did to try to get me to throw a skill I was afraid of. Sometimes I just couldn't find it within myself. One time when I was feeling defeated, Heather, my beam coach approached me. She was very patient and looked past my fear and spoke straight to the little girl who was panicking inside. Like I was a child of her own who had scraped her knee, she simply told me that I was ok, and I'll never forget the hug she gave me. When it was time for me to try again, instead of letting my brain wander to my fear, I repeated to myself the same things I had been just been told. I thought about the first step of that skill and thought through the second, third and final step. When I listened to the guidance that came from my coaches, I always found some kind of a breakthrough.

One of the most important things my coaches taught me how to do was breathe. Remembering to breathe helps keep you from falling apart and helps you think clearly. Even as an athlete today, I still remind myself to do this so I don't get overcome by fear or anxiety and stress myself out. Learning how to comfort yourself is an important trait to have in life. It's how you become resilient when you are feeling overwhelmed, because someone else won't always be there to do it. Eventually you will grow up and encounter difficult things, and if you can talk yourself out of panicking, the truth that you tell yourself will keep you moving. A truth you would never have learned if not for the love and support of a parent, teacher, or coach.

Reflect

Describe a time when your coach/parent comforted you when you were afraid.

What did they say that helped you?

When you comfort yourself, what do you tell yourself?

Fight or Flight

Fight or Flight

Whenever I get overwhelmed or stressed about something, my initial instinct is to freak out, especially during physical exercise. I hate that I do this! It's one of those things I know does zero good for me, but I do it anyway. By definition, the fight or flight response is described as follows:

The response of the sympathetic nervous system to a stressful event, preparing the body to fight or flee, associated with the adrenal secretion of epinephrine and characterized by increased heart rate, increased blood flow to the brain and muscles, raised sugar levels, sweaty palms and soles, dilated pupils, and erect hairs.

Throughout my years of being an athlete, I have asked myself the same question. When there is an option to fight, why do I immediately take flight? I think when I am working out and getting beat by my workout, I feel like the victim to something that is happening to me. If I am a victim, than I am not in control and I am helpless. To me, there is nothing worse than feeling like there is nothing you can do to change a bad situation. When you're in flight mode, it's like the walls are caving in on you and cutting off your supply to air at the same time. When it's happening, it's kind of like experiencing predetermined regret.

Usually I am not the kind of person that gets mad. Certain things irritate me and other things rub me the wrong way, but few things make me angry. That's a part of the problem. When you're a victim, you don't get mad at what is happening to you, because you don't know you have the right to be. As it slowly dawns on you that what is happening isn't fair, you suddenly see the injustice of it all and you have an emotional response of outrage. No one changes their situation when they feel helpless, but only when their eyes are opened to what should not be happening. After years of being dominated by stress, worry and doubt during physical exercise, it's time to become someone new. Now is the time to finally take back the right to succeed! Because it belongs to me. When I start to feel overcome, it's time to get mad at the thought of being manipulated by stress and push back! To better sum it up,

It's time to go beast mode!

Reflect

How do you respond to a stressful situation?

Describe a time when you felt like you were being controlled by stress.

How could you have controlled your stress, instead of letting your stress control you?

Negativity

"Mental toughness takes practice. The more you practice, the stronger you will be when you face the next fear."
-Jessica Cunningham-

Negativity

Most of my dreams don't make sense, but I had a dream last night that made me think about something I have overlooked. In the dream, I was in high school P.E. on a day we were supposed to run the track. No one was looking forward to it. In fact everyone was dreading it. At first I let my peer's UN-enthusiasm influence me and for a minute, I hated running just as much as they did. When I started running, however, I realized I was good at it, and before I knew it, I was lapping my peers with tons of energy to spare. Curious to see what else I could do, I found an open field away from everyone and I began to tumble. I have had plenty of dreams of tumbling in the past, but this time, my tumbling felt different. It was free from thought or judgment or negativity. Anything that popped in my head to do, I did without effort. I'll never forget the feeling of my body rising into the air as if it knew no height or the feeling of hitting the perfect shapes to weightlessly twist and flip. The dream ended with me in the middle of this field, holding the longest handstand I have ever done. Beyond loving the sensation of throwing my body around, I loved being without the negativity that surrounded my peers.

After having this dream, it occurred to me that negativity keeps us earth-bound. Like many athletes do today, I fought negative thoughts my entire gymnastics career. In fact, the majority of my practices were spent fighting negative thoughts. It always seemed like I would temporarily convince myself to stay positive, but just as soon as the negative thoughts left, they would always come right back to the surface and take away my chance to succeed. When I believed in myself, I experienced completing a skill successfully, but the minute I started doubting myself, slowly I would digress from my capabilities and find myself mentally trapped in my box, doubting myself. I assumed this was and would always be a never-ending battle. I didn't realize at the time, that it didn't have to be.

If I know anything about negativity today, it's that it is a heavy burden to carry. You don't have to walk many steps before growing tired from the weight of it resting on your shoulders. Think of it like a barbell with bags of loaded garbage hanging from either end that you have to haul on your back through the desert. Even though the idea of carrying this trash around in the hot, hot sun doesn't make sense, many of us choose to struggle with our trash when we could continue on without it. It's the same thing with training: If I could let go of all negativity during my workouts, I know I would wildly progress beyond my expectations. It sounds easy to do, but it is actually quite difficult and requires practice. Sometimes when I notice I am struggling because of the negative thoughts in my head, I have to stop wherever I am and get rid of them before I can go on. Even if that means I don't finish my assignment as quickly, I have to re-train my brain to get rid of the negativity versus trying to struggle and work with it. It is one thing to go through a mental block over something specific, but constantly trying to work with negativity on your mind is one of the most destructive ways to train. Even the idea of training with it should not be entertained.

Athletes need many things in order to become great: determination, courage, perseverance, but negativity is NOT one of them. Mentally dragging negativity around will only hold us back from what we need to get done and we won't get to experience our highest potential.

Reflect

What are the thoughts that keep you from doing a skill? What are the negative words that you fight?

What are 3 positive words you can replace the negative words with?

What could/will you accomplish without negativity?

Struggles

"If there is no struggle,
There is no progress."
-Fredrick Douglas-

Struggles

There is a famous fact that is often quoted in fitness. You are your worst enemy. As a young athlete, I remember bargaining, fighting and talking in my head. While recently training in Crossfit, I was reminded how easily I default to mentally beating myself up. Even though over critiquing myself is a bad thing, it is usually a good sign that I am making progress. Think about it, if you get to the point in your training where you don't have to strain your effort, mentally, or physically, you're probably not pushing yourself enough, or you're probably ready to move on to the next level.

Sometimes success can sneak up on you because of how easy it is to get caught up in your own head. For me, that battle looks like over critiquing myself to the point where I slow down my progression. If my coach doesn't make me move on, occasionally I will re-do skills over and over again because I think they are too terrible to count. When you are pushing yourself, your only thoughts are those of survival. Personally, these thoughts are: "Only three more", or "Just breathe". Somewhere along the way I have to dig deep to find the motivation to keep going, even though it feels like I don't have anything left. Sometimes we assume that having to struggle is a negative thing, like it makes us weak. In actuality, struggling makes us stronger, more intentional people. Have you ever noticed that when you are struggling, you are more focused and driven? I am. It's like determination gets the better of me and all I want to do is whatever it is that I can't. Where normally I would skip over the things that challenge me, I tackle them head on, because I want to succeed.

Over time, whether I notice it right away or not, my hard work does pay off. In the future, the things that used to challenge me, I can do and the new things that are challenging me I never would have been able to do in the past. It just comes down to looking at the whole picture instead of staring at the immature cracks that your struggle has yet to fill. Struggle doesn't mean we are unequipped to handle our circumstance, it only means that we are being molded into better athletes and people. If we can be patient with ourselves and remember that, maybe struggling wouldn't affect us to such a negative degree. If we just allow ourselves time to struggle with our challenges, progression might even come faster.

When it is time to move on, we will do so with more strength and endurance than ever before!

Reflect

What is something you are currently struggling with?

How can struggling with this make you a stronger athlete and person in the future?

The Ugly Truth

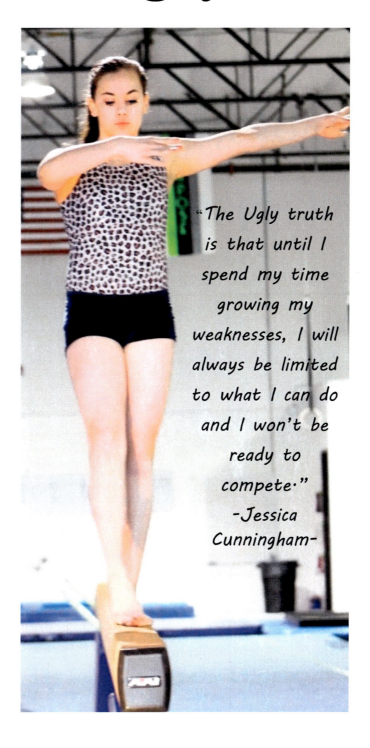

"The Ugly truth is that until I spend my time growing my weaknesses, I will always be limited to what I can do and I won't be ready to compete."
-Jessica Cunningham-

The Ugly Truth

I don't like to admit it, but as a gymnast, I was a terrible competitor! Even though I wanted to be, I was not the gymnast who had it all together. I loved to train because there was less pressure and I could easily do what I loved in peace. For various reasons, the minute I stepped onto the competition floor, I would simply fall apart. I can remember when I would look around at the skills other gymnasts were doing and totally feel out of place, like I didn't deserve to be called a level 10. So consequently, I competed as if I didn't have anything to offer. Other times, I wouldn't be able to control my nerves and my nervousness would get the best of me. But I wonder sometimes what really made me so nervous. Was it the pressures of competition or was it because of my training?

It always feels good to train the skills you are good at. It confirms that you are talented and it boosts your self-esteem. For me, a few of the skills I was good at included Tkatchev's releases on bars, double lay-out dismount off bars, and double anything tumbling passes on floor. Those were some of my favorite skills to work on in the gym. These were also the skills that were in my routines because they were what we wanted to showcase to the judges in competition. On the other hand, skills involving twisting? I didn't twist unless it was out of a double lay-out dismount off bars. That was the only place I ever successfully twisted. I never figured out how to twist out of a regular tumbling pass (front or back) from any other apparatus. I was labeled a flipper, not a twister. My flipping came naturally because I could jump and I was fast twitched. I trained a vault called the Yurchenko for a short time, only to discover that I was too fast onto the table and flipped off too close to the end of the table. Once we closed the door on that vault, it limited what else I could do in that event. Towards the end of my career was a race against time, as I was attempting to get a scholarship for college. Consequently, determining what would be in my routines depended on how quickly I learned the skills or how naturally the skill came to me.

In gymnastics, there are so many skills. It is difficult to master them all, but if I had mastered more by paying more attention to the skills I was weak at, would I have felt like I was just a one-trick pony? If I could go back and change anything in my gymnastics career, it would be to focus on what challenged me the most. Today, as a retired gymnast who now has a second chance to face my weakness, I am choosing to work on the skills in Crossfit that challenge me the most. The hardest thing about doing that is a temporary slowing of my progress. In fact, it has slowed down to the point that I am finishing my work outs dead last. I have a competition coming up soon and the first WOD (Workout Of the Day) contains three of the things I struggle with the most in the gym. To prepare me, my coach has created workouts centered around those weaknesses. Let me be the first to say that it has doubled the meaning of what I thought it was to be challenged. One thing that hasn't changed about me as an athlete is how nervous I get when I perform. Just thinking about my competition has made me as nervous as if I were already there. I have even had re-occurring dreams about gymnastics meets where I let my team down and completely humiliate myself because of my limitations in a competition.

As I go to that dark place in my workouts where I am haunted by the same feeling of inadequacy I had as a gymnast, I realize in that moment, I am not ready. At first the thoughts makes me panic and I get lost in discouragement, but the ugly truth is that until I spend my time growing my weakness, I will always be limited to what I can do and won't be ready to compete. The philosophy to get me ready to compete has changed from stringing a series of things I am good at into a routine, to building up the things I need to work on by attacking my weaknesses. I am a good athlete, but if I want to improve, I have to be great at what comes naturally to me and be willing to perfect what doesn't. If I train with this kind of purpose, I will become the athlete I was meant to become. It will just take going through fire to get there

Reflect

What are some of your weaknesses?

How could you strengthen your weaknesses?

Insecurities

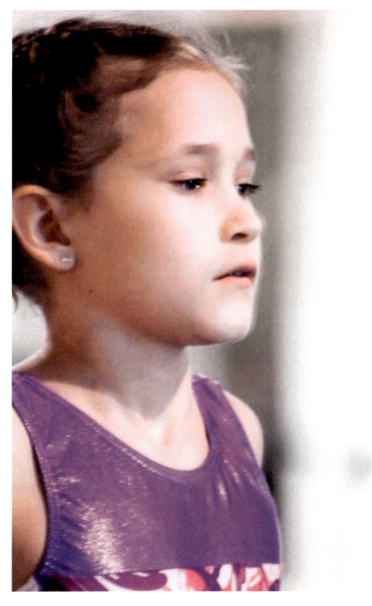

"Remember that you were perfectly made and cannot be compared to anyone else."
-Jessica Cunningham-

Insecurities

We all struggle with being insecure about something. That something usually involves not being _____ enough. Fill in the blank. For me, it's not being big enough. Growing up, I tried many different activities and most of them weren't short-person friendly. More than anything in the world, I hate to be called small or tiny or little because despite my five foot, 105 pound stature, I have never really felt small a day in my life. In this lifetime, I want to do big things and make a big difference, so I have always had big dreams. When someone says I am small, I hear that I am not big enough and I let that insecurity weigh on the shoulders of what I want to do or become. The fear of being too small to want big things in life is my insecurity monster and everyone has one. But why?

When you think about it, the answer is simple. We, as humans, were designed for greatness and every one of us has the potential to be great, so naturally there is an enemy who tries to stop us from reaching our capabilities because we are a threat. The enemy can be the media who tells you how you should look, or someone who can't handle that you are better than they are, or even our own thoughts as we compare ourselves to other people. But whatever it is that the enemy is telling you, remember that you were perfectly made and cannot be compared to anyone else. The dreams you have and the intricate way you were designed fits you like a puzzle piece. Shrug off the need to compare yourself to another person who is meant for something completely different because there is no comparison. You are made without mistake! With that in mind, we all have something important to offer the world, but if we try to force ourselves to be like someone else or fit our neighbors destiny, we will actually create more insecurities and frustrations for ourselves and fulfill less of what we were meant to do.

Instead of letting someone else make you feel inadequate, use them to motivate you. When someone tells me I am small, the words I tell myself are, "I'll show you small!" Then I work that much harder to prove them wrong, because I believe I was made for big things. As real as they feel to us, our insecurities are simply lies that we believe are true. The truth is that once we discover how to overcome our own insecurities, out of a darkness that was once ruled by our own doubt, we will be unstoppable!

The enemy should be afraid!

Reflect

What insecurities does your insecurity monster feed off of? (Physical appearance, size, etc.)

What do you believe you were meant for?

What makes you special? Name 3 things you like about yourself.

Score Chasing

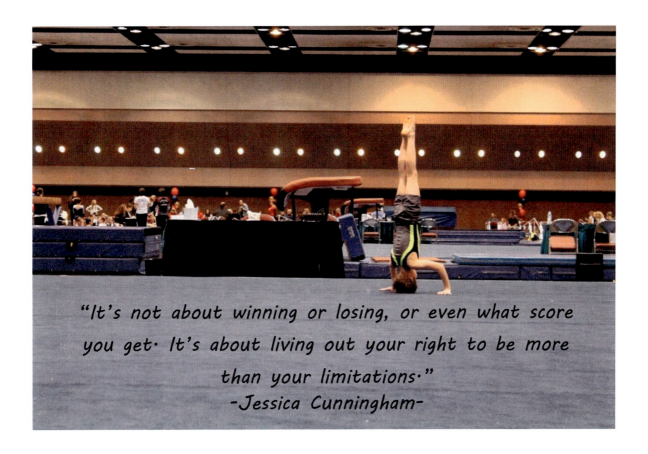

"It's not about winning or losing, or even what score you get. It's about living out your right to be more than your limitations."
-Jessica Cunningham-

Score Chasing

Have you ever thought about why athletes do what they do? Think about it. Most high-level athletes train up to 30+ hours a week and sacrifice a normal life because of their dedication to their sport. They work through injuries they shouldn't and daily risk injury by challenging themselves to be better. But why? Loving a sport means that you accept the bad things that come along with the good, because there are always unpleasant factors that follow wearing your body down. While I was in gymnastics, some of the less enjoyable parts included having hands that looked and felt like I was a logger, constantly fighting joint pain, and rest? What's that? Why put your body through all of that? For some athletes, it's for a college scholarship, for others it's all they know, some athletes even have goals to go to the Olympics. For me, however, a lot of the reason I put myself through so much pain was because I wanted a good score. Even though it sounds a bit silly, getting a good score is about one of the only rewards gymnasts get for their hard work. When athletes win or get a good score, it validates all the things they tolerate and makes their sacrifice a little more worthwhile. No matter which way you slice it, gymnasts are score chasers, which makes them perfectionists by default because they only win or get a good score by staying close to perfection. Along with many other concepts to figure out in Crossfit, training and competing without scoring ranks in the top five. I often find myself thinking,

"If I'm not getting a 9.5 or higher, then why am I pushing my body so hard?"

In general, my goal for myself is to improve by testing my boundaries and breaking through limits I have set for myself. Even though it's not easy, pushing myself gives me a sense of purpose and proves that I am made of more than I thought. Similar to gymnastics, Crossfit fulfills my desire to achieve new heights, but in a different way. I am not doing it for perfection or for a score, I am doing it for the right to be limitless. I believe I was designed to be something bigger than my limitations.

Although I have a reason to push myself, I still find myself chasing a score, even when there isn't one to chase. The perfectionist in me wants the overall goal to be attained. Receiving a medal or a high score appeased that part of me in the past. But maybe that part of me can be happy with receiving an artificial score for meeting mental goals. Instead of being recognized for being perfect, maybe I can be judged on my ability to go unbroken or go until failure more often. It might be a bit unorthodox, but getting a score is what makes sense to me, so temporarily training this way might help me progress faster. At some point, my reason to push through won't be perfection anymore, it will be about living out my goals instead.

Reflect

Does winning or getting a high or low score tell you what kind of an athlete you are? Why or why not?

What kind of mental goals could you come up with that would help you?

The Pain of Change

The Pain of Change

Have you ever lost motivation to do something you really want? About a month ago I decided to make it a goal to go to regionals in Crossfit. I'm thinking it will take me about two years or more to be ready for that, but I am already overwhelmed. I know I have a lot of work to do, and the thought of how far I need to go is intimidating. Today during my workout I found that I was unmotivated to push myself because I am so far from accomplishing that goal. I know I should be looking at this one day at a time, but I've never attempted to do anything this big. For the first time in my life I feel small, and I don't know how someone as small as me can achieve a goal as big as mine.

It's one thing to say you want to do something, but when you feel the weight of what that requires, it's something completely different. In gymnastics, I wanted to train elite to attempt to make it to the Olympics, but I didn't make it that far. I never experienced the physical demand or having to constantly push. Change hurts. It takes more determination, more sweat and more will power to go past where you have been. More than failure, what scares me the most about changing is that I will succeed. I've never been a friend of change. I like to know what everything will be like before I do it. When life gets too unpredictable, I am immediately anxious because venturing out into the unknown is serious business. There is a lot of risk involved that pulls you away from what you consider safe. Among other things I will be risking my comfort, my convenience, and my time on this adventure, and I won't come out the same.

But at the same time, I don't want to be left unchanged. I don't want to waste a single day choosing to be less because it's easier. If I can respect where I am in my journey, get up after a bad day and push through the pain of change, I can persevere through anything. Doing these things won't leave me average. They will make me exceptional because of my choice to fight through what most people give up on every day. I will not give up. No matter how badly change tries to scare me away from my dream, I will not settle for easy or comfortable. Will you?

Moving forward on our journey will require that we throw out all expectation of what we think is waiting for us in the future. It's not going to be hard, it's going to be costly. You will have to put your whole heart and spirit into your desire to succeed. You will need to learn to love the slow grind and leave those behind who keep you from success. This journey will not be like any other, because this journey is about to get real.

Reflect

How do you feel about change? Does it scare you? Do you like it?

 Although it is logical to value comfort, sometimes wanting to be comfortable can keep you from pushing in your workouts. How important is it to you to be comfortable?

Another Me

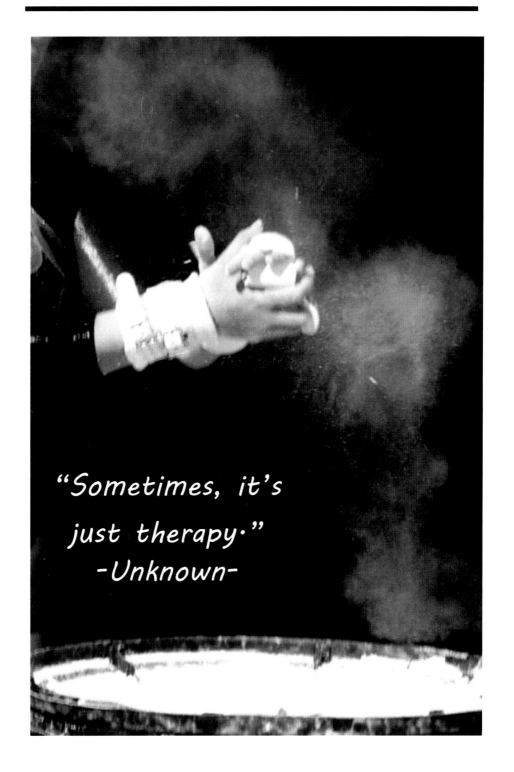

"Sometimes, it's just therapy."
-Unknown-

Another Me

I am not very good at being honest with my emotions. No matter how I am feeling, I always try to make it look like I have it all together. The truth is sometimes I don't, and pretending like I do drives me to be unsure of how to act around people. I tire myself out trying to behave a certain way.

When I retired from gymnastics, the hardest part for me was emotionally and mentally replacing who I thought I was. I had been a gymnast for so long that I had forgotten there was more to me than that. I didn't know that confusing my identity was so easy because for years, my sport was all I did. However, I have learned that being an athlete isn't all I am. It's only a part of me.

After retiring, I was free to return to a normal life, but I had lost the main way I processed what I was feeling. Being on the beam, locked in the zone, was just what I needed sometimes. When the world around me felt like it was caving in, focusing became my getaway. When I was young, a terrible thing happened to me. At the age of 10, I lost my mom to breast cancer. Besides the obvious reasons for being emotionally stressed, losing my mom was hard because she was the one who put me in gymnastics in the first place. Gymnastics was our thing and losing her felt like losing a part of me. I continued gymnastics after she passed away, but I struggled to focus and had an even harder time performing. I went through a phase where I didn't really want to talk to anybody, and if I did, I didn't talk about what was going on inside. Although I was shaken by this heart-breaking life event, something I didn't expect happened.

I can remember it exactly. I was really out of it during practice one day and we had gone to floor to tumble. We began to go through a warm-up that I usually struggled with. Before I started, I closed my eyes and imagined that I was in another world with my mom in it. Imagining her with me was the only thing I could do that would keep me going. Without my usual hesitations and doubt, I simply let go and threw my body into a new confidence I had never tapped into before. And I flew. On the outside it probably just looked like I was fast and that I could jump high, but on the inside it felt like I was tumbling fast enough to catch her and jumping high enough to reach her. In that moment, I didn't care what it looked like. My main concern wasn't that my tumbling was perfect; my main concern was that I could express what I was feeling in a way that I couldn't say. I will always remember that day. I became powerful enough to do what I normally wouldn't and learned that my mom would always be with me.

What makes athletes amazing to me, is their ability to focus. There can be loud cheering and even louder music around them, but if they are truly focused, they won't hear a single voice or sound. It's like mentally they go to another place where they are protected from their everyday worries. When they are truly focused, they slow down the world around them, and envision a new one in its place. Their concentration covers them like a shield. This is the place I found peace and beauty in being who I was, not only as an athlete, but also as a person. I discovered I was strong, driven, brave, loyal, dedicated, powerful, focused, beautiful and talented. Focusing my world away gave me great freedom to just be myself.

It's important for athletes to have an outside outlet. Whether that be through another passion or a session of open gym in their sport, athletes need time to confront their emotions. Similar to artists, I have known athletes to be very passionate people who feel things magnified. When life hits us with turmoil, we are affected to the core. Most of us bottle up our stress and never release the pressure, but eventually, we will reach our limit and we will explode. But if we are dealing with our emotions on a regular basis, we will be able to focus ourselves into a new world where we are invincible.

Reflect

Describe a time you went through something emotionally difficult?

What helped you through it?

Fill in the blank… When I am feeling overwhelmed with my emotions I can deal with them by:

The Why

"Being an athlete is not who I am, it is what God has gifted me to do. Doing what I believe I was made for gives me the purpose I need to train hard in order to be great.
This is why I am an athlete."
-Jessica Cunningham-

The Why

Do you ever stop and think about why you do what you do? If you're a dedicated athlete, you sacrifice a lot to be where you are in your sport. When you could be hanging out with your friends or sleeping, you put all the energy you have left into your training. More than being the best or winning, there has to be an internal motive. The internal motive is what gets you to train on days you don't feel like leaving the house. It's the reason you work so hard and strive to be the best. Internal motivation is linked to the spirit. The human spirit is a strong thing. Some people call it pride or egotism, but for the athlete who uses their whole heart, mind, and body, it is their spirit that leads them through. Without a strong spirit, there is no passion to pursue, no will to win, no determination to succeed. For me, it is my spirit that tells me to try again after I have failed and keeps me pushing past discomfort. It's the feeling I get from doing what I love that ultimately brings me back for more. When my spirit is fed by my passion, a fire is lit and all of my senses are awakened as if seeing or hearing for the first time. The surge that races through me sparks every muscle to fire and joins every nerve together and for an instant, I feel the most alive I have ever felt. In these moments, I am filled with excitement and energy, but most importantly, I am filled with hope. Hope that I can make it through anything. Doing what you love is highly underestimated these days, but when you dedicate yourself to that thing you love, you walk into a completely different world.

Beyond the satisfaction I get from doing what I love, I do what I do because of my faith. Sometimes I look up at the stars and smile because of how breathtakingly gorgeous they are. I am inspired by the stars because they remind me that they exist to shine, and that I should too. I can't help but be grateful thinking that every star in the sky and every planet that fascinates me was made for me, and yet I am more valuable than they are to the God who created them. As I fulfill what I was made for and use my gifts and live for those passions that have been given to me, I am just as beautiful as those stars I look up at every night.

When you think about the miracle of creation and how God spoke every galactic mystery into existence with a single word and then moved on to create us in His own image, you start to realize that there is more to our composition than happenstance. What an honor to be able to reflect the creator of Saturn's rings with our abilities. Our greatness represents our great God, and as long as I believe in Him, there will never be anything I can't do.

Crossfit is not who I am, it is what God has gifted me to do. Doing what I believe I was made for gives me the purpose I need to train as hard as I do in order to be great.

This is why I Crossfit.

Reflect

Why do you do what you do?

Loving the Journey

"Every bit of growth in the gym is a success and deserves to be pridefully acknowledged."
-Jessica Cunningham-

Loving the Journey

Competitions are strange to me. No matter how hard you train and sacrifice, when it's time to prove yourself during a competition, anything can throw you off. I see a lot of people who get overwhelmed with disappointment after competing. I remember that feeling. I recall thinking all my hard work was for nothing because of my performance. But was it really?

Anyone who focuses on becoming the best will tell you that winning is great. And it is. But more important than what you do, or don't do in a competition, is that you enjoy the trip that brought you there. Remember all the times you made mental breakthroughs or executed a skill by yourself for the very first time? What about the moment when you fell in love with conditioning, even though it's awful. Or the time you took a hard fall and then decided not to let that fall determine your capability? The list can go on and on. When it comes down to it, the journey to becoming the best is more valuable than getting a trophy that says you're the best. The journey is overlooked, but it's what gets you out of bed every day and gives you a sense of purpose. The time you spend in the gym is rewarded by what you accomplish every day, both as an athlete and a person. The most difficult practices are the ones that shape you the most, and even though you look back on them and groan, you smile when you think about how far you stand above them now. Athletes who only love competitions love them because they believe that is when they're supposed to shine. If they love competing, they should love training ten times more. Without all the hours of training, athletes wouldn't be able to compete in the first place. If you love your training, your image of yourself won't be changed by whether or not you get a medal.

If you were to go into a house where a child's height was measured in marks on the wall, you wouldn't just be seeing a pattern of ascending height. You would also be seeing growth in other things not shown on the wall, like character and intelligence. If the child came out to show you all the times he grew, he would do it with pride right? Than so should the athlete who has put in the effort to progress. Every bit of growth in the gym is a success and deserves to be pridefully acknowledged. A trophy doesn't describe what you feel when you are in the gym, and it definitely doesn't describe what you are worth. If athletes thought about their training this way, or kept track of their victories, their cheap piece of medal wouldn't tell them what to feel. Your training is what makes you beautiful. Even last place should not take away your pride, because it's not about the destination, it's about the journey.

Reflect

Think about your career in your sport. Describe your best memories and why those memories are important to you.

How do you feel about your training? Do you love it? Why?

How do you feel about competing? Do you love it? Why?

Swimming in the Deep End

Swimming in the Deep End

I hate to swim. I freak out a little when I get into the deep water. I don't like that I can't stop when I get tired, when I reach the point of no return and the only way to get to the other side is to keep going. In the shallow end, I'm enjoying moving in the water. I like swimming there because I can play. But the minute I venture out where I can't touch the bottom, my perception of the water changes from positive to negative. Most pools have some kind of slope or drop off into the deep end, and my athletic career isn't any different.

As I am organizing plans to make it to regionals in Crossfit, I have found myself standing in front of a drop off. Behind me is a version of me I have known for years. This version of me has shown great strength and endured more than I thought I could have and mentally achieved many breakthroughs. She has brought me where I am today and helped me become the athlete that I am. Looking back on what I have achieved is satisfying, and if I'm honest, looking forward into what I have yet to achieve is scary. Becoming an elite athlete is what I have wanted to be since I was a child, but now that I am finally training to become that, I am hesitant. I can't help but wonder if I should go back to the shallow end, where I know I will succeed. If I turn around now, I won't be risking failure. If I swim out into the deep end, I will be surrounded by all kinds of failures. Workouts would be easier if I stayed in the shallow end. I would have less to stress about, but I would question whether I did the right thing for years down the road and wonder how far I could have gone. I want to push off the ground beneath me and swim into the unknown, but I haven't yet. So far, I've just been staring into the deep waters ahead of me, feeling unequipped to make it to the other side.

I often put too much pressure on myself to the point where I feel overwhelmed. Two good friends told me something today that is very valuable. They said that even though the end goal is regionals, the first step is tomorrow. After that, is the next day, and after that is the next day. I have to take one day at a time and do what is going to help me get to my goal that day. They are right. I don't have to swim to the other side right now, I just have to get to the first flotation device and move on to the next one after that and gradually make my way to the end by taking small steps forward. Thinking about my goal like this helps me to manage the journey better and encourages me to push away from the shallow end and swim. So that is what I am going to do. I'm going to do what I can today and worry about tomorrow when it comes. That's all I really can do. So I say goodbye to the old me who taught me about my abilities and prepared me for this grand take off. This is where we part ways. What I learned in the shallow end of my career has been essential, but it's time for me to make my move and learn to swim in the deep end.

Reflect

What is the ultimate goal for you in your sport? How far do you want to go?

What can you do today that will help you get there? Make it a point to ask yourself this question every day. By taking one day at a time, you will be closer to your goal than you ever thought you could be.

Belief and Confidence

Belief and Confidence

What would you say if I told you that you had a super power? Better than flying or shooting lasers from your eyes, your power allows you to shape shift into whoever you want to be and shake the ground beneath you like thunder.

Let me guess, when you were a child, you made strange things happen right? But when you decided to tell the world about what you could do, the world brushed you off and convinced you to believe in an explanation more logical. So you did. After years of thinking logically, your power began to fade and eventually you learned how to doubt. With every passing day that you don't live by this power inside you, you lose confidence until you are as average as the world wanted you to become. However, when you lie down to sleep at night, images of a lustrous golden light keep you awake. Normally you wouldn't think anything of it, but you're seeing these images on a regular basis and you somehow feel a connection to them. What could this be? Could it be your imagination or could it be a memory? Curious to find out, you hold your breath and quietly peel back your covers. Being careful not to wake anyone, you slide into a pair of pants with holes in them, pull a hoody over your head and sneak out the window by your bed. While standing in the glow of the moonlight, you can hear everything. Every cricket that chirps, every owl that hoots, and the rustling of the wind blowing through the trees. There is no one around you. It crosses your mind to be afraid, but then you realize that you are finally free to re-discover something you've believed in from the time you were a child. Straight ahead there is a river with a small boat waiting at its shore. You cross the grass to get to it and push off and paddle into the middle of the river. There isn't any time to waste, so right away you close your eyes and concentrate on the light. As your mind scans through its archive of memories, it finds something. Not only do you see the light again, you feel it warm your body from the inside out. The light gets brighter and the heat gets warmer until you open your eyes. What you see takes your breath away and you stare in disbelief. Surrounding you is a globe of the light with depictions of a future you on

112

its walls. You are more powerful than ever and whatever you focus on bends to your belief in it. Is it real? It all seems like another dream. The globe slowly dissipates while you decide and soon it is gone. Stunned, you sit in your boat for a while and reflect on what you have seen.

In reality, there is no way to see what you are capable of in the future. But we do have a super power. Belief is a powerful thing. Brought on by positivity, believing in yourself produces a confidence that changes the fate of your dreams. If you're an athlete, you know that different challenges present themselves when you are trying to be the best at something. These challenges are what separate the athletes who are faint of heart from the athletes who are willing to do whatever it takes and believe they can overcome anything. When I look inside myself and see me facing my biggest weakness in the gym, I don't always believe I can do it. More than anything I do physically in Crossfit, believing in myself is both my biggest struggle and my secret weapon. There is usually a large portion of my heart that wants to fully believe, but an even bigger area that doesn't know how.

What I admire most about children is their ability to believe. Once children are told about something magical they don't doubt its existence or need proof. They simply use their God-given ability to make their belief real. As we age, we all get more and more realistic about what we should believe in and what we shouldn't. Somehow we have given ourselves the authority to deem what is possible and what we can achieve. But who has the right to put a border around you? If you believe you can do something, there is no telling how far your faith in yourself will carry you. Most athletes are too used to limiting their future and need to re-train their hearts and minds in how to be confident again. The past couple of weeks, I have spent the car ride to Crossfit repeating positive statements to myself. I say things like,

"I am strong and fearless."

"Even if I fail, I'll get right back up and leave my failure behind."

"Nothing will stand in my way."

"Roar."

Saying these things to myself is a way I can fill my head and heart with belief to succeed. When I don't believe in myself and I talk negatively to myself, I am setting myself up to fail and my performance is a failure. But when I talk positively to myself, I start to build confidence and prepare myself to start behaving like a champion. The more I think like a champion, the more I train like one and the more I train like a confident champion, the closer I come to being one. Too often I see athletes making goals without confidence or with little belief that they will actually achieve their dreams. If you want to do something, no matter how big or how small, say it out loud and then claim that desire by saying,

"I am going to do _____." Fill in the blank.

At first you might feel uncomfortable with this new mindset, but just know that you need to be that confident in order to be the best. Use your super power of belief to shake the world around you as you ignite your light and change the world forever. Whatever you want to do or become in your life is already yours. You just have to believe in yourself the way a child has faith in the unseen.

Reflect

When you talk to yourself, what do you say? Is it positive or is it negative?

What is your positive statement? Do you have one? If not, create one.

What is it you are going to set out to do? What is the dream that you are going to make a reality?

Photo Gallery

"Today I will do what others won't so tomorrow I can do what others can't."
- Unknown-

"Breathe in every detail of every moment."
-Jessica Cunningham-

"This is what I was created to do. I was made to excel and to achieve. I am so ready for this."
-Jessica Cunningham-

Tranquility fueled by Fire.

"Concentration is my shield from my everyday worries. When I am completely focused, I am invincible."
-Jessica Cunningham-

"Anything worth fighting for is going to be difficult. But having to fight for it doesn't make it any less worth it."
-Jessica Cunningham-

"Any kind of progress requires a leap of faith."
-Jessica Cunningham-

Jessica Cunningham lives in Portland Oregon with her dog-child, Lacey. She coaches compulsory gymnastics and trains to compete in Crossfit. To learn more about Jessica, go to
www.Jessicacunningham.net

Made in the USA
Coppell, TX
16 January 2024